Beginning Level

LEARNING TO LISTEN IN ENGLISH

Virginia Nelson

National Textbook Company
a division of *NTC Publishing Group* • Lincolnwood, Illinois USA

For Jeanne Nelson

About the Author

Virginia Nelson is a lecturer in the Summer Session ESL Program at Cornell University and a curriculum writer for a Title VII science-based whole literacy program in Tempe, Arizona.

Acknowledgments

I want to thank these people for their contributions to *Learning to Listen in English:* Barbara Cramer, Daniel Rivas, Luis Francisco Rivas, Luis José Rivas, Professor Carlos Vallejo, and Zhang Jian Rong.

Illustrations by Don Wilson
Cover design by Linda Snow Shum
Design by Sara Shelton
Audio production by Phyllis Dolgin

Published by National Textbook Company, a division of NTC Publishing Group.
© 1997 by NTC Publishing Group, 4255 West Touhy Avenue,
Lincolnwood (Chicago), Illinois 60646-1975 U.S.A.

7 8 9 ML 0 9 8 7 6 5 4 3 2 1

Contents

Unit 1: Letters and Numbers

Name _____

Letters

PART 1

A B C D E F G H I J K L M
a b c d e f g h i j k l m

↓ A B C **B**____   I J K ____   I K M ____
a b c **b**____   i j k ____   i k m ____

B C D ____   J K L ____   B D F ____
b c d ____   j k l ____   b d f ____

C D E ____   K L M ____   D F H ____
c d e ____   k l m ____   d f h ____

D E F ____   A C E ____   F H J ____
d e f ____   a c e ____   f h j ____

E F G ____   C E G ____   H J L ____
e f g ____   c e g ____   h j l ____

F G H ____   H G I ____   J L A ____
f g h ____   h g i ____   j l a ____

H I J ____   G I K ____
h i j ____   g i k ____

PART 2

Name _____

N O P Q R S T U V W X Y Z
n o p q r s t u v w x y z

↓ N O P **P**   V W X ____   V X Z ____
n o p **p**   v w x ____   v x z ____

O P Q ____   W X Y ____   Z O Q ____
o p q ____   w x y ____   z o q ____

P Q R ____   X Y Z ____   O Q S ____
p q r ____   x y z ____   o q s ____

Q R S ____   N P R ____   Q S U ____
q r s ____   n p r ____   q s u ____

R S T ____   P R T ____   S U W ____
r s t ____   p r t ____   s u w ____

T U V ____   R T V ____   U W Y ____
t u v ____   r t v ____   u w y ____

U V W ____   T V X ____
u v w ____   t v x ____

Name _____

U.S. Cities

A Atlanta

B Boston

C Chicago

D Denver

E El Paso

F Fort Worth

G Green Bay

H Houston

I Indianapolis

J Jacksonville

K Kansas City

L Los Angeles

M Miami

N New York City

O Orlando

P Portland

R Richmond

S San Francisco

T Topeka

W Washington, D.C.

Y Youngstown

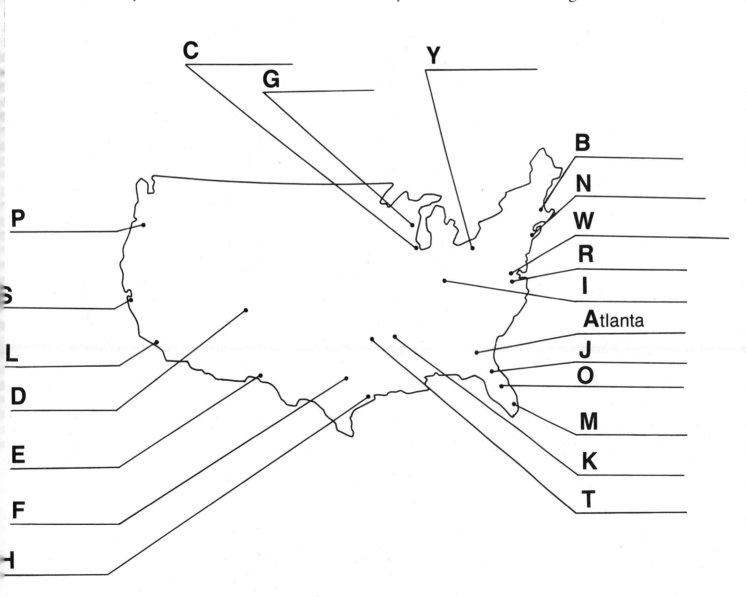

Name _____

Numbers

1 2 3 4 5 6 7 8 9 10

↓
1	2	3	_3_
2	3	4	_____
3	4	5	_____
3	2	1	_____
4	3	2	_____
5	4	3	_____
1	3	5	_____

2	4	5	_____
5	3	1	_____
5	4	2	_____
6	7	8	_____
7	8	9	_____
8	9	10	_____
8	7	6	_____

9	8	7	_____
10	9	8	_____
6	8	10	_____
7	9	10	_____
10	8	6	_____
10	9	7	_____

11 12 13 14 15 16 17 18 19 20

11	12	13	_11_
12	13	14	_____
13	14	15	_____
13	12	11	_____
14	13	12	_____
15	14	13	_____
1	11	2	_____
2	12	3	_____

3	13	4	_____
4	14	5	_____
5	15	1	_____
16	17	18	_____
17	18	19	_____
18	19	20	_____
18	17	16	_____

19	18	12	_____
20	19	18	_____
6	16	7	_____
7	17	8	_____
8	18	9	_____
9	19	10	_____
10	20	6	_____

Name _____

More Numbers

PART 1

20   30   40   50   60   70   80   90   100

20	30	40	_30_	2	12	20	____	100	90	80	____
30	40	50	____	3	13	30	____	16	60	17	____
40	50	60	____	4	14	40	____	17	70	18	____
40	30	20	____	5	15	50	____	18	80	19	____
50	40	30	____	1	10	11	____	19	90	16	____
60	50	40	____	60	70	80	____	6	16	60	____
12	20	2	____	70	80	90	____	7	17	70	____
13	30	14	____	80	90	100	____	8	18	80	____
14	40	15	____	80	70	60	____	9	19	90	____
15	50	11	____	90	80	70	____	1	10	100	____

PART 2

21   32   43   54   65   76   87   98

21	43	65	87	98
_22_	____	____	____	____
____	72	____	____	____
____	____	____	____	____
____	____	____	____	98
31	____	____	80	____
____	55	65	____	____
____	____	____	____	____
____	____	____	____	____

Name _____

Temperatures

1. Atlanta	86°F	30°C	Atlanta	**86°F**	**30°C**	
2. Boston	86°F	30°C	Boston	_____	_____	
3. Chicago	89°F	32°C	Chicago	_____	_____	
4. Denver	81°F	27°C	Denver	_____	_____	
5. El Paso	98°F	37°C	El Paso	_____	_____	
6. Fort Worth	93°F	34°C	Fort Worth	_____	_____	
7. Green Bay	83°F	28°C	Green Bay	_____	_____	
8. Houston	90°F	32°C	Houston	_____	_____	
9. Indianapolis	87°F	31°C	Indianapolis	_____	_____	
10. Jacksonville	94°F	34°C	Jacksonville	_____	_____	
11. Kansas City	86°F	30°C	Kansas City	_____	_____	
12. Los Angeles	79°F	26°C	Los Angeles	_____	_____	
13. Miami	86°F	30°C	Miami	_____	_____	
14. New York City	90°F	32°C	New York City	_____	_____	
15. Orlando	97°F	36°C	Orlando	_____	_____	
16. Portland	82°F	28°C	Portland	_____	_____	
17. Richmond	89°F	32°C	Richmond	_____	_____	
18. San Francisco	65°F	18°C	San Francisco	_____	_____	
19. Topeka	87°F	31°C	Topeka	_____	_____	
20. Washington, D.C.	89°F	32°C	Washington, D.C.	_____	_____	
21. Youngstown	91°F	33°C	Youngstown	_____	_____	

Name _____

World Cities

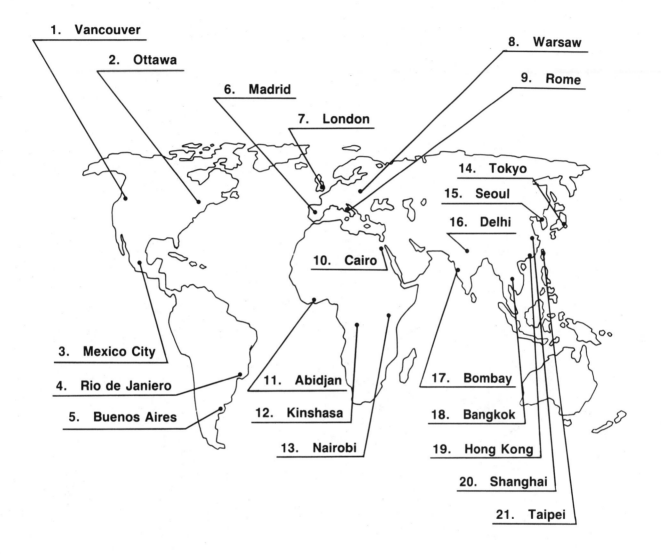

1. Vancouver

2. Ottawa

6. Madrid

7. London

8. Warsaw

9. Rome

14. Tokyo

15. Seoul

16. Delhi

10. Cairo

3. Mexico City

4. Rio de Janiero

5. Buenos Aires

11. Abidjan

12. Kinshasa

13. Nairobi

17. Bombay

18. Bangkok

19. Hong Kong

20. Shanghai

21. Taipei

1. __Vancouver__

2. _____

3. _____

4. _____

5. _____

6. _____

7. _____

8. _____

9. _____

10. _____

11. _____

12. _____

13. _____

14. _____

15. _____

16. _____

17. _____

18. _____

19. _____

20. _____

21. _____

Name _____

Continents

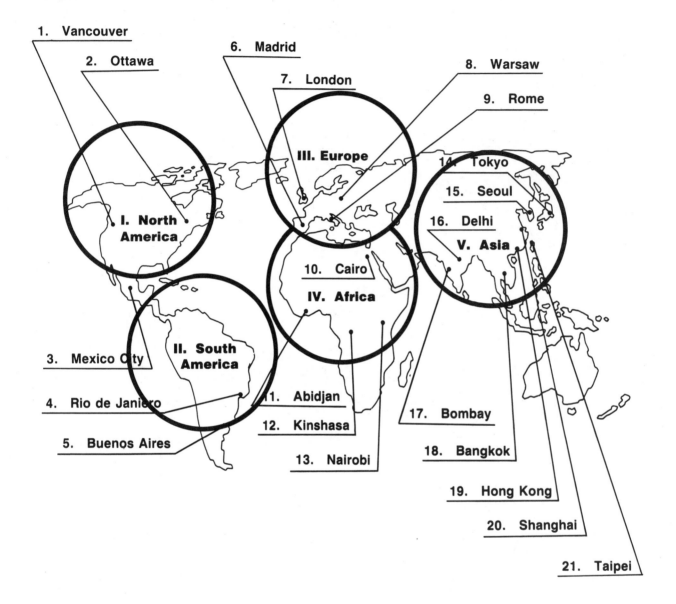

1. Vancouver
2. Ottawa
6. Madrid
7. London
8. Warsaw
9. Rome
14. Tokyo
15. Seoul
16. Delhi
V. Asia
III. Europe
I. North America
3. Mexico City
4. Rio de Janiero
5. Buenos Aires
II. South America
10. Cairo
IV. Africa
11. Abidjan
12. Kinshasa
13. Nairobi
17. Bombay
18. Bangkok
19. Hong Kong
20. Shanghai
21. Taipei

I. _____North America_____

II. _____

III. _____

IV. _____

V. _____

North America

1. __Vancouver_____

2. _____

3. _____

South America

4. _____

5. _____

Europe

6. _____

7. _____

8. _____

9. _____

Africa

10. _____

11. _____

12. _____

13. _____

Asia

14. _____

15. _____

16. _____

17. _____

18. _____

19. _____

20. _____

21. _____

Name _____

Cities and Continents

1. Vancouver is in North America. _____
2. _____
3. _____
4. _____
5. _____
6. _____
7. _____
8. _____
9. _____
10. _____
11. _____
12. _____
13. _____
14. _____
15. _____
16. _____
17. _____
18. _____
19. _____
20. _____
21. _____

Name _____

Continents, Cities, and Temperatures

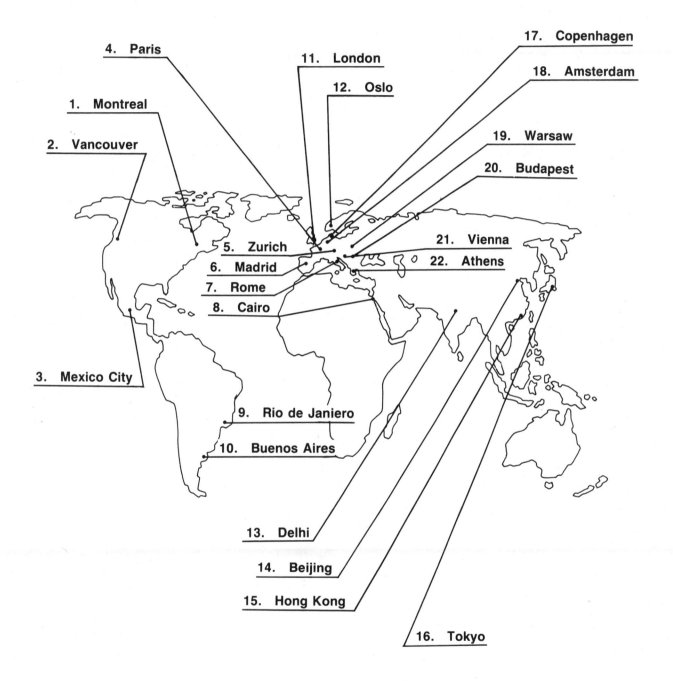

4. Paris

11. London

12. Oslo

17. Copenhagen

18. Amsterdam

19. Warsaw

20. Budapest

1. Montreal

2. Vancouver

5. Zurich

6. Madrid

7. Rome

8. Cairo

21. Vienna

22. Athens

3. Mexico City

9. Rio de Janiero

10. Buenos Aires

13. Delhi

14. Beijing

15. Hong Kong

16. Tokyo

	Continent	City	Temperature
1.	North America	Montreal	91°F
2.			
3.			
4.			
5.			
6.			
7.			
8.			
9.			
10.			
11.			
12.			
13.			
14.			
15.			
16.			
17.			
18.			
19.			
20.			
21.			
22.			

Unit 2: Clock Time

Name _____

Hours

PART 1

12:00

_____

_____

_____

_____

_____

_____

_____

_____

_____

_____

_____

Name _____

  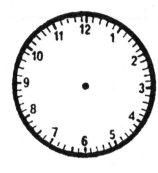 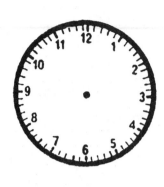

12:00 _____ 1:00 _____ _____ _____

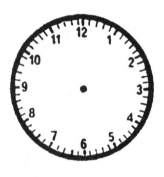  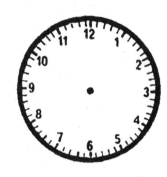 

_____ _____ _____ _____

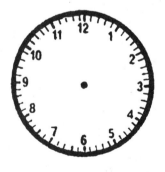 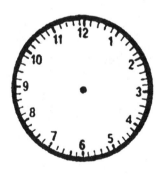 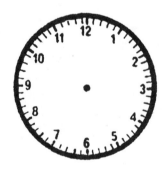 

_____ _____ _____ _____

Name _____

Half Hours

12:30 _____   _____   _____   _____

_____   _____   _____   _____

_____   _____   _____   _____

Name _____

12:30

1:30

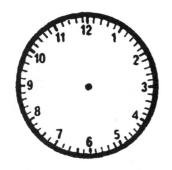

Name _____

Quarter Hours

   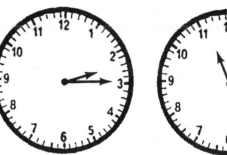

12:15 _____ _____ _____ _____

_____ _____ _____ _____

_____ _____ _____ _____

Name _____

12:15   1:15

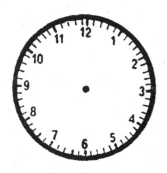 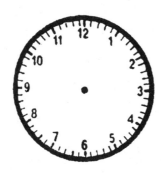 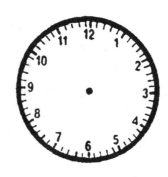 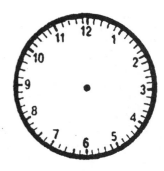

 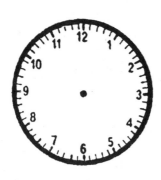  

Name _____

More Quarter Hours

PART 1

  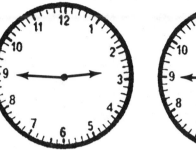 

12:45 _____   _____   _____   _____

_____   _____   _____   _____

_____   _____   _____   _____

Name _____

→

12:45 _____   1:45 _____   _____   _____

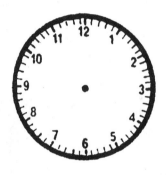      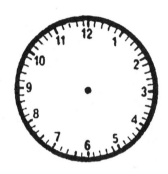   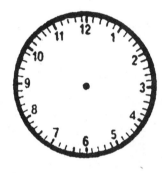

_____   _____   _____   _____

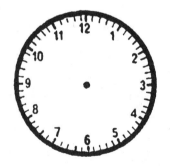         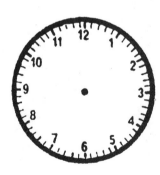

_____   _____   _____   _____

Minutes

PART 1

12:05 _____

Name _____

12:05   1:10   _____   _____

  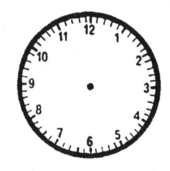 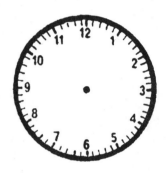

_____   _____   _____   _____

  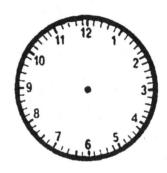 

_____   _____   _____   _____

Name _____

Writing the Time

1. ___1:00___   21. _____

2. _____   22. _____

3. _____   23. _____

4. _____   24. _____

5. _____   25. _____

6. _____   26. _____

7. _____   27. _____

8. _____   28. _____

9. _____   29. _____

10. _____   30. _____

11. _____   31. _____

12. _____   32. _____

13. _____   33. _____

14. _____   34. _____

15. _____   35. _____

16. _____   36. _____

17. _____   37. _____

18. _____   38. _____

19. _____   39. _____

20. _____   40. _____

Activities

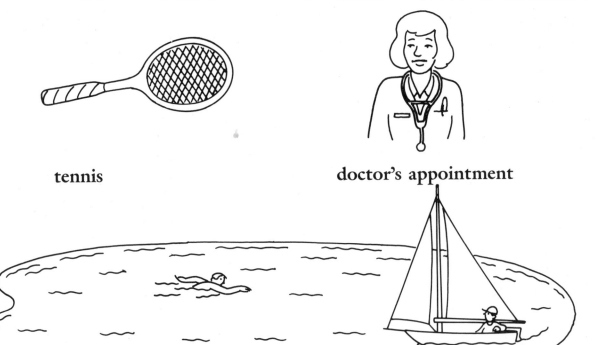

tennis

doctor's appointment

swimming

sailing

dentist's appointment

baseball

fishing

lunch

Name _____

Agenda

8:00	fishing _____
8:30	_____
9:00	_____
9:30	_____
10:00	_____
10:30	_____
11:00	_____
11:30	_____
12:00	_____
12:30	_____
1:00	_____
1:30	_____
2:00	_____
2:30	_____
3:00	_____
3:30	_____
4:00	_____
4:30	_____
5:00	_____

Name _____

Sample Agendas

Dana

8:00 fishing _____

9:00 _____

10:00 _____

11:00 _____

12:00 lunch _____

1:00 _____

2:00 _____

3:00 _____

4:00 _____

Richard

8:00 _____

9:00 _____

10:00 _____

11:00 _____

12:00 _____

1:00 _____

2:00 _____

3:00 _____

4:00 _____

Steve

8:00 _____

9:00 _____

10:00 _____

11:00 _____

12:00 _____

1:00 _____

2:00 _____

3:00 _____

4:00 _____

Yasuko

8:00 _____

9:00 _____

10:00 _____

11:00 _____

12:00 _____

1:00 _____

2:00 _____

3:00 _____

4:00 _____

Name _____

More Agendas

		Activity	Time
Dana:	1.	fishing	7:00
	2.		
	3.		
	4.		
Richard:	5.		
	6.		
	7.		
	8.		
Steve:	9.		
	10.		
	11.		
	12.		
Yasuko:	13.		
	14.		
	15.		
	16.		

Name _____

Bus Timetable 1

Leaving	
Albuquerque	12:00
Atlanta	1:00
Boston	2:30
Chicago	3:45
Los Angeles	4:15
New York City	5:00

Arriving	
Denver	8:15
New Orleans	11:05
New York City	7:45
Cleveland	11:00
San Francisco	1:45
Washington, D.C.	10:30

Name _____

Bus Timetable 2

Leaving		Arriving	
1. Albuquerque	2:00	Los Angeles	5:00
2.			
3.			
4.			
5.			
6.			
7.			
8.			
9.			
10.			
11.			
12.			
13.			
14.			
15.			
16.			
17.			
18.			
19.			
20.			
21.			
22.			

Unit 3: Calendar Time

Name _____

Days of the Week

PART 1

| Sunday | Monday | Tuesday | Wednesday | Thursday | Friday | Saturday |

1. Sunday   _____Sunday_____

2. Monday   _____

3. Tuesday   _____

4. Wednesday _____

5. Thursday _____

6. Friday   _____

7. Saturday _____

PART 2

Sunday	_____Monday_____	Tuesday
Monday	_____	Wednesday
Tuesday	_____	Thursday
Wednesday	_____	Friday
Thursday	_____	Saturday
Friday	_____	Sunday
Saturday	_____	Monday

Name _____

Days of the Week with <u>After</u>, <u>Before</u>, and <u>Between</u>

after   Saturday   <u>Sunday</u>

             Sunday   _____

             Monday   _____

             Tuesday   _____

             Wednesday   _____

             Thursday   _____

             Friday   _____

before   <u>Saturday</u>   Sunday

            _____   Monday

            _____   Tuesday

            _____   Wednesday

            _____   Thursday

            _____   Friday

            _____   Saturday

between   Saturday   <u>Sunday</u>   Monday

             Tuesday   _____   Thursday

             Friday   _____   Sunday

             Monday   _____   Wednesday

             Thursday   _____   Saturday

             Wednesday _____   Friday

             Sunday   _____   Tuesday

Months of the Year

PART 1

January	February	March	April	May	June
July	August	September	October	November	December

1. January   <u>   January   </u>

2. February   _____

3. March   _____

4. April   _____

5. May   _____

6. June   _____

7. July   _____

8. August   _____

9. September   _____

10. October   _____

11. November   _____

12. December   _____

PART 2

January	<u>February</u>	March	_____
February	_____	April	_____
March	_____	May	_____
April	_____	June	_____
May	_____	July	_____
June	_____	August	_____
July	_____	September	_____
August	_____	October	_____
September	_____	November	_____
October	_____	December	_____

Name _____

Months of the Year with <u>After</u>, <u>Before</u>, and <u>Between</u>

PART 1

after

January	<u>February</u>
February	_____
April	_____
June	_____
August	_____
November	_____

PART 2

before

<u>March</u>	April
_____	February
_____	November
_____	June
_____	August
_____	January

PART 3

between

January	<u>February</u>	March
May	_____	July
September	_____	November
April	_____	June

Name _____

The Calendar

January							February							March							April						
S	M	T	W	T	F	S	S	M	T	W	T	F	S	S	M	T	W	T	F	S	S	M	T	W	T	F	S
					1	2		1	2	3	4	5	6		1	2	3	4	5							1	2
3	4	5	6	7	8	9	7	8	9	10	11	12	13	6	7	8	9	10	11	12	3	4	5	6	7	8	9
10	11	12	13	14	15	16	14	15	16	17	18	19	20	13	14	15	16	17	18	19	10	11	12	13	14	15	16
17	18	19	20	21	22	23	21	22	23	24	25	26	27	20	21	22	23	24	25	26	17	18	19	20	21	22	23
24	25	26	27	28	29	30	28	29						27	28	29	30	31			24	25	26	27	28	29	30
31																											

May							June							July							August						
S	M	T	W	T	F	S	S	M	T	W	T	F	S	S	M	T	W	T	F	S	S	M	T	W	T	F	S
1	2	3	4	5	6	7			1	2	3	4						1	2		1	2	3	4	5	6	
8	9	10	11	12	13	14	5	6	7	8	9	10	11	3	4	5	6	7	8	9	7	8	9	10	11	12	13
15	16	17	18	19	20	21	12	13	14	15	16	17	18	10	11	12	13	14	15	16	14	15	16	17	18	19	20
22	23	24	25	26	27	28	19	20	21	22	23	24	25	17	18	19	20	21	22	23	21	22	23	24	25	26	27
29	30	31					26	27	28	29	30			24	25	26	27	28	29	30	28	29	30	31			
														31													

September							October							November							December						
S	M	T	W	T	F	S	S	M	T	W	T	F	S	S	M	T	W	T	F	S	S	M	T	W	T	F	S
				1	2	3							1		1	2	3	4	5						1	2	3
4	5	6	7	8	9	10	2	3	4	5	6	7	8	6	7	8	9	10	11	12	4	5	6	7	8	9	10
11	12	13	14	15	16	17	9	10	11	12	13	14	15	13	14	15	16	17	18	19	11	12	13	14	15	16	17
18	19	20	21	22	23	24	16	17	18	19	20	21	22	20	21	22	23	24	25	26	18	19	20	21	22	23	24
25	26	27	28	29	30		23	24	25	26	27	28	29	27	28	29	30				25	26	27	28	29	30	31
							30	31																			

1. January has ___31___ days.

2. February has _____ days.

3. March has _____ days.

4. April has _____ days.

5. May has _____ days.

6. June has _____ days.

7. July has _____ days.

8. August has _____ days.

9. September has _____ days.

10. October has _____ days.

11. November has _____ days.

12. December has _____ days.

How Long Are the Months?

January								February								March								April						
S	M	T	W	T	F	S		S	M	T	W	T	F	S		S	M	T	W	T	F	S		S	M	T	W	T	F	S
					1	2			1	2	3	4	5	6			1	2	3	4	5								1	2
3	4	5	6	7	8	9		7	8	9	10	11	12	13		6	7	8	9	10	11	12		3	4	5	6	7	8	9
10	11	12	13	14	15	16		14	15	16	17	18	19	20		13	14	15	16	17	18	19		10	11	12	13	14	15	16
17	18	19	20	21	22	23		21	22	23	24	25	26	27		20	21	22	23	24	25	26		17	18	19	20	21	22	23
24	25	26	27	28	29	30		28	29							27	28	29	30	31				24	25	26	27	28	29	30
31																														

May								June								July								August						
S	M	T	W	T	F	S		S	M	T	W	T	F	S		S	M	T	W	T	F	S		S	M	T	W	T	F	S
1	2	3	4	5	6	7					1	2	3	4							1	2		1	2	3	4	5	6
8	9	10	11	12	13	14		5	6	7	8	9	10	11		3	4	5	6	7	8	9		7	8	9	10	11	12	13
15	16	17	18	19	20	21		12	13	14	15	16	17	18		10	11	12	13	14	15	16		14	15	16	17	18	19	20
22	23	24	25	26	27	28		19	20	21	22	23	24	25		17	18	19	20	21	22	23		21	22	23	24	25	26	27
29	30	31						26	27	28	29	30				24	25	26	27	28	29	30		28	29	30	31			
																31														

September								October								November								December						
S	M	T	W	T	F	S		S	M	T	W	T	F	S		S	M	T	W	T	F	S		S	M	T	W	T	F	S
				1	2	3								1			1	2	3	4	5						1	2	3
4	5	6	7	8	9	10		2	3	4	5	6	7	8		6	7	8	9	10	11	12		4	5	6	7	8	9	10
11	12	13	14	15	16	17		9	10	11	12	13	14	15		13	14	15	16	17	18	19		11	12	13	14	15	16	17
18	19	20	21	22	23	24		16	17	18	19	20	21	22		20	21	22	23	24	25	26		18	19	20	21	22	23	24
25	26	27	28	29	30			23	24	25	26	27	28	29		27	28	29	30					25	26	27	28	29	30	31
								30	31																					

31 Days   **30 Days**   **28 or 29 Days**

_____ January _____   _____   _____

_____   _____

_____   _____

_____   _____

_____

_____

Name _____

Days and Dates

January	February	March	April
S M T W T F S	S M T W T F S	S M T W T F S	S M T W T F S
1 2	1 2 3 4 5 6	1 2 3 4 5	1 2
3 4 5 6 7 8 9	7 8 9 10 11 12 13	6 7 8 9 10 11 12	3 4 5 6 7 8 9
10 11 12 13 14 15 16	14 15 16 17 18 19 20	13 14 15 16 17 18 19	10 11 12 13 14 15 16
17 18 19 20 21 22 23	21 22 23 24 25 26 27	20 21 22 23 24 25 26	17 18 19 20 21 22 23
24 25 26 27 28 29 30	28 29	27 28 29 30 31	24 25 26 27 28 29 30
31			

May	June	July	August
S M T W T F S	S M T W T F S	S M T W T F S	S M T W T F S
1 2 3 4 5 6 7	1 2 3 4	1 2	1 2 3 4 5 6
8 9 10 11 12 13 14	5 6 7 8 9 10 11	3 4 5 6 7 8 9	7 8 9 10 11 12 13
15 16 17 18 19 20 21	12 13 14 15 16 17 18	10 11 12 13 14 15 16	14 15 16 17 18 19 20
22 23 24 25 26 27 28	19 20 21 22 23 24 25	17 18 19 20 21 22 23	21 22 23 24 25 26 27
29 30 31	26 27 28 29 30	24 25 26 27 28 29 30	28 29 30 31
		31	

September	October	November	December
S M T W T F S	S M T W T F S	S M T W T F S	S M T W T F S
1 2 3	1	1 2 3 4 5	1 2 3
4 5 6 7 8 9 10	2 3 4 5 6 7 8	6 7 8 9 10 11 12	4 5 6 7 8 9 10
11 12 13 14 15 16 17	9 10 11 12 13 14 15	13 14 15 16 17 18 19	11 12 13 14 15 16 17
18 19 20 21 22 23 24	16 17 18 19 20 21 22	20 21 22 23 24 25 26	18 19 20 21 22 23 24
25 26 27 28 29 30	23 24 25 26 27 28 29	27 28 29 30	25 26 27 28 29 30 31
	30 31		

Sunday   Monday   Tuesday   Wednesday   Thursday   Friday   Saturday

January 20   <u>Wednesday</u>   March 2   _____

February 15   _____   November 6   _____

August 1   _____   May 30   _____

July 4   _____   October 31   _____

December 25   _____   April 10   _____

Dana's Calendar of Events

M A R C H

S	M	T	W	T	F	S
		1	2	3	4	5 ① 2:30 fishing
6 ② 6:00 tennis	7	8	9	10	11	12
13 ③ 4:15 swimming	14	15	16	17	18	19 ④ 3:15 baseball
20	21 ⑤12:45 lunch with Yasuko	22	23	24	25 ⑥ 9:30 sailing	26 ⑦12:45 dentist's appointment
27	28	29	30	31 ⑧11:15 doctor's appointment		

	Activity	Date	Time
1.	fishing	March 5	2:30
2.			
3.			
4.			
5.			
6.			
7.			
8.			

Name _____

Richard's Calendar of Events

S	M	T	W	T	F	S
1	**2**	**3** ②	**4**	**5**	**6**	**7**
8	**9**	**10**	**11**	**12** ③	**13**	**14** ④
15 ⑤	**16**	**17**	**18**	**19**	**20**	**21** ⑥
22 ⑦	**23**	**24**	**25**	**26**	**27**	**28** ⑧
29 ① 1:00 sailing	**30**	**31**				

M A Y

	Activity	Date	Time
1.	sailing	May 29	1:00
2.			
3.			
4.			
5.			
6.			
7.			
8.			

Name _____

Steve's Calendar of Events

\\multicolumn{7}{c}{**A U G U S T**}						
S	M	T	W	T	F	S
	1 2:00 sailing	2	3	4	5	6
7	8	9	10	11	12	13
14	15	16	17	18	19	20
21	22	23	24	25	26	27
28	29	30	31			

Activity	Date	Time
1. sailing	August 1	2:00
2. _____	_____	_____
3. _____	_____	_____
4. _____	_____	_____
5. _____	_____	_____
6. _____	_____	_____
7. _____	_____	_____
8. _____	_____	_____

Name _____

Yasuko's Calendar of Events

			J U L Y			
S	M	T	W	T	F	S
					1	2 6:15 fishing
3	4	5	6	7	8	9
10	11	12	13	14	15	16
17	18	19	20	21	22	23
24	25	26	27	28	29	30
31						

	Activity	Date	Time
1.	fishing	July 2	6:15
2.			
3.			
4.			
5.			
6.			
7.			
8.			

Unit 4: Money

ACTIVITY A

Name _____

Dollars

1 dollar
$1.00
$1

5 dollars
$5.00
$5

10 dollars
$10.00
$10

1. ___$1___

2. _____

3. _____

4. _____

5. _____

6. _____

7. _____

8. _____

9. _____

10. _____

11. _____

12. _____

13. _____

14. _____

15. _____

16. _____

17. _____

18. _____

Cents

a quarter	a dime	a nickel	a penny
25 cents	10 cents	5 cents	1 cent
25¢	10¢	5¢	1¢
$.25	$.10	$.05	$.01

1. ____$.25____   11. _____   21. _____

2. _____   12. _____   22. _____

3. _____   13. _____   23. _____

4. _____   14. _____   24. _____

5. _____   15. _____   25. _____

6. _____   16. _____   26. _____

7. _____   17. _____   27. _____

8. _____   18. _____   28. _____

9. _____   19. _____   29. _____

10. _____   20. _____   30. _____

Name _____

Dollars and Cents

$10.15 _____

_____

_____

_____

_____

_____

_____

_____

_____

_____

_____

_____ →

$1.06

Name _____

Train Information

Destination	Departure Time	Fare
1. New York City	8:30	$239
2.		
3.		
4.		
5.		
6.		
7.		
8.		
9.		
10.		

Unit 5: The Planets

Name _____

The Planets

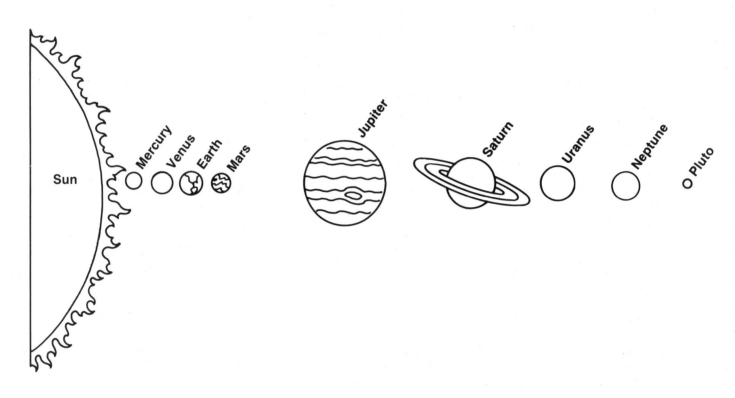

1. Mercury   <u>Mercury</u>

2. Venus   _____

3. Earth   _____

4. Mars   _____

5. Jupiter   _____

6. Saturn   _____

7. Uranus   _____

8. Neptune   _____

9. Pluto   _____

Name _____

Bigger and Smaller

Pluto Mercury Mars Venus Earth Neptune Uranus Saturn Jupiter

Smaller

1. __Pluto_____ Mercury
2. _____ Mars
3. _____ Venus
4. _____ Earth
5. _____ Neptune
6. _____ Uranus
7. _____ Saturn
8. _____ Saturn
9. _____ Jupiter
10. _____ Jupiter

Bigger

11. __Jupiter_____ Saturn
12. _____ Uranus
13. _____ Neptune
14. _____ Earth
15. _____ Venus
16. _____ Mars
17. _____ Mercury
18. _____ Pluto
19. _____ Pluto
20. _____ Mercury

Name _____

Sentences with <u>Bigger</u> and <u>Smaller</u>

1. _____Pluto_____ is smaller than Mercury.

2. _____ is smaller than Mars.

3. _____ is smaller than _____.

4. _____ is smaller than _____.

5. _____ is smaller than _____.

6. _____ is smaller than _____.

7. _____ is smaller than _____.

8. _____ is smaller than _____.

9. _____ is _____ than _____.

10. _____ is _____ than _____.

11. _____ is _____ than _____.

12. _____ is _____ than _____.

13. _____ is bigger than Saturn.

14. _____ is bigger than Uranus.

15. _____ is bigger than Neptune.

16. _____ is bigger than _____.

17. _____ is bigger than _____.

18. _____ is bigger than _____.

19. _____ is bigger than _____.

20. _____ is bigger than _____.

21. _____ is bigger than _____.

22. _____ is _____ than _____.

23. _____ is _____ than _____.

24. _____ is _____ than _____.

Name _____

Closer to and Farther from

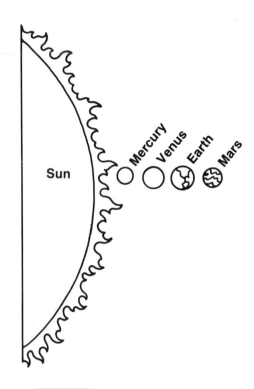 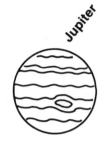 

PART 1

PART 2

Closer to

Farther from

1. _Mercury_____ Venus

2. _____ Earth

3. _____ Mars

4. _____ Jupiter

5. _____ Saturn

6. _____ Uranus

7. _____ Neptune

8. _____ Pluto

9. _____ Pluto

10. _____ Pluto

11. _Pluto_____ Neptune

12. _____ Uranus

13. _____ Saturn

14. _____ Jupiter

15. _____ Mars

16. _____ Earth

17. _____ Venus

18. _____ Mercury

19. _____ Mercury

20. _____ Mercury

Name _____

Sentences with <u>Closer to</u> and <u>Farther from</u>

1. _____Mercury_____ is closer to the sun than Venus.

2. _____ is closer to the sun than Earth.

3. _____ is closer to the sun than Mars.

4. _____ is closer to the sun than Jupiter.

5. _____ is closer to the sun than _____.

6. _____ is closer to the sun than _____.

7. _____ is closer to the sun than _____.

8. _____ is _____ _____ the sun than _____.

9. _____ is _____ _____ the sun than _____.

10. _____ is _____ _____ the sun than _____.

11. _____ is farther from the sun than Neptune.

12. _____ is farther from the sun than Uranus.

13. _____ is farther from the sun than Saturn.

14. _____ is farther from the sun than Jupiter.

15. _____ is farther from the sun than _____.

16. _____ is farther from the sun than _____.

17. _____ is farther from the sun than _____.

18. _____ is _____ _____ the sun than _____.

19. _____ is _____ _____ the sun than _____.

20. _____ is _____ _____ the sun than _____.

Name _____

Numbers

PART 1

→ 100 __110__ _____ _____ _____ _____ _____

200 _____ _____ 300 _____ _____ 400 _____

500 _____ 600 _____ 700 _____ 800 _____

900 _____

1. __927__   16. _____   31. _____

2. _____   17. _____   32. _____

3. _____   18. _____   33. _____

4. _____   19. _____   34. _____

5. _____   20. _____   35. _____

6. _____   21. _____   36. _____

7. _____   22. _____   37. _____

8. _____   23. _____   38. _____

9. _____   24. _____   39. _____

10. _____   25. _____   40. _____

11. _____   26. _____   41. _____

12. _____   27. _____   42. _____

13. _____   28. _____   43. _____

14. _____   29. _____   44. _____

15. _____   30. _____   45. _____

Name _____

→ 1,000   __**2,000**__   3,000   _____   5,000   _____

6,000   _____   7,000   _____   8,000   _____

9,000   _____   10,000   _____   12,000   _____

13,000   _____   15,000

20,000   _____   40,000   _____   60,000   _____

80,000   _____

1.   __**1,234**__   16.   _____

2.   _____   17.   _____

3.   _____   18.   _____

4.   _____   19.   _____

5.   _____   20.   _____

6.   _____   21.   _____

7.   _____   22.   _____

8.   _____   23.   _____

9.   _____   24.   _____

10.   _____   25.   _____

11.   _____   26.   _____

12.   _____   27.   _____

13.   _____   28.   _____

14.   _____   29.   _____

15.   _____   30.   _____

Name _____

→ 100,000 _____**200,000**_____ 300,000 _____ 500,000 _____

700,000 _____ 900,000

1,000,000 _____ 3,000,000 _____

5,000,000 _____ 7,000,000 _____

9,000,000 _____ 11,000,000 _____

20,000,000 _____ 40,000,000 _____

60,000,000 _____ 80,000,000 _____

100,000,000 _____ 300,000,000 _____

1. _____**125,435**_____   11. _____

2. _____   12. _____

3. _____   13. _____

4. _____   14. _____

5. _____   15. _____

6. _____   16. _____

7. _____   17. _____

8. _____   18. _____

9. _____   19. _____

10. _____   20. _____

Name _____

Distances

1,000,000,000   2,000,000,000   3,000,000,000

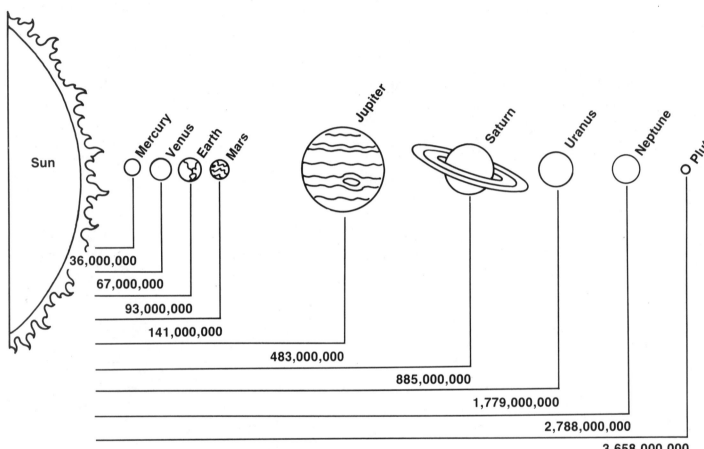

36,000,000

67,000,000

93,000,000

141,000,000

483,000,000

885,000,000

1,779,000,000

2,788,000,000

3,658,000,000

1. Mercury is _____ 36,000,000 _____ miles from the sun.

2. Venus is _____ miles from the sun.

3. _____ is _____ miles from the sun.

4. _____ is _____ miles from the sun.

5. Jupiter is 483,000,000 miles from the sun. _____

6. _____

7. _____

8. _____

9. _____

Name _____

Diameter

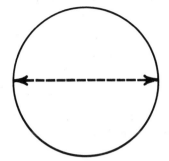

Pluto 1,860
Mercury 3,026
Mars 4,208
Venus 7,504
Earth 7,909
Neptune 30,690
Uranus 32,116
Saturn 74,400
Jupiter 88,536

1. The diameter of Mercury is _____ 3,026 _____ miles.

2. The diameter of _____ is _____ miles.

3. The diameter of _____ is _____ miles.

4. ___The diameter of Mars is 4,208 miles._____

5. _____

6. _____

7. _____

8. _____

9. _____

ACTIVITY I

Order

Sun   Mercury   Venus   Earth   Mars   Jupiter   Saturn   Uranus   Neptune   Pluto

| first | second | third | fourth | fifth | sixth | seventh | eighth | ninth |
| 1st | 2nd | 3rd | 4th | 5th | 6th | 7th | 8th | 9th |

PART 1

1. Mercury is the _____ first _____ planet from the sun.

2. Venus is the _____ planet from the sun.

3. _____ is the _____ planet from the sun.

4. _____ is the _____ planet from the sun.

5. __Jupiter is the fifth planet from the sun._____

6. _____

7. _____

8. _____

9. _____

PART 2

1. The _____ first _____ planet is Mercury.

2. The _____ planet is Venus.

3. The _____ planet is _____.

4. The _____ planet is _____.

5. __The fifth planet is Jupiter._____

6. _____

7. _____

8. _____

9. _____

Unit 6: Food

Name _____

Food

PART 1

corn

bread

muffin

celery

cheese

carrots

tomato

apple

eggs

ice cream

hamburger

hot dog

Name _____

_____ corn _____   _____   _____

 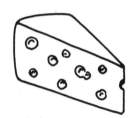 

_____   _____   _____

_____   _____   _____

  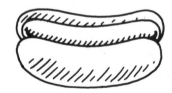

_____   _____   _____

Name _____

Alphabetical Order

apple   _____

bread   _____ bread _____

carrots   _____ carrots _____

celery   _____

cheese   _____

corn   _____

eggs   _____

hamburger   _____

hot dog   _____

ice cream   _____

muffin   _____

tomato   _____

Name _____

Breakfast, Lunch, and Dinner

Breakfast	Lunch	Dinner
eggs	hot dog	hamburger
bread	carrots	muffin
	celery	cheese
	apple	corn
		tomato
		ice cream

Breakfast	Lunch	Dinner
eggs		
_____	_____	_____
_____	_____	_____
	_____	_____
	_____	_____
		_____

Dana

1. Dana has eggs and bread for breakfast.

2. She has a hamburger and a carrot for _____lunch_____.

3. For dinner, she has a tomato, celery, a _____, and

   _____.

Richard

4. Richard has a _____ and a tomato for _____.

5. He has a _____, corn, and cheese for _____.

6. For _____, he has a hamburger and _____.

Steve

7. Steve has a hot dog for _____.

8. He _____.

9. For _____.

Yasuko

10. Yasuko _____.

11. _____.

12. _____.

Name _____

Menus

	Dana	Richard	Steve	Yasuko
apples	✔		✔	✔
bread				
carrots				
celery				
cheese				
eggs				
hamburgers				
hot dogs				
ice cream				
muffins				
tomatoes				

More Foods

PART 1

coffee

fish

bananas

pear

potato

tortillas

orange

beans

milk

strawberries

rice

squash

Name _____

_____ coffee _____   _____   _____   _____

_____   _____   _____   _____

_____   _____   _____   _____

Name _____

At the Supermarket

apples	$ .29
bananas	$ .33
beans	$ .79
bread	$1.25
carrots	$ .88
celery	$ .89
cheese	$2.04
coffee	$3.49
corn	$ .18
eggs	_____
fish	_____
hamburgers	_____
hot dogs	_____
ice cream	_____
milk	_____
muffins	_____
oranges	_____
pears	_____
potatoes	_____
rice	_____
squash	_____
strawberries	_____
tomatoes	_____
tortillas	_____

Name _____

Breakfast Menu for the Week

Sunday

milk
_____
bread
_____
coffee
_____

Monday

_____

_____

_____

Tuesday

_____

_____

_____

Wednesday

_____

_____

_____

Thursday

_____

_____

_____

Friday

_____

_____

_____

Saturday

_____

_____

_____

Lunch Menu for the Week

Sunday

_____ fish

_____ rice

_____ tortillas

_____ bananas

Monday

_____

_____

_____

_____

Tuesday

_____

_____

_____

_____

Wednesday

_____

_____

_____

_____

Thursday

_____

_____

_____

_____

Friday

_____

_____

_____

_____

Saturday

_____

_____

_____

_____

Name _____

Dinner Menu for the Week

Sunday	Monday	Tuesday
corn	_____	_____
carrots	_____	_____
eggs	_____	_____
milk	_____	_____

Wednesday	Thursday	Friday
_____	_____	_____
_____	_____	_____
_____	_____	_____
_____	_____	_____

Saturday

_____

_____

_____

_____

Name _____

Restaurant Menu

Breakfast

2 eggs and a muffin, bread, or tortillas   ____$3.25____

Juice

     Apple, tomato, orange   small   ___$ .65___

                                medium   _____

                                large   _____

Milk, coffee   small   _____

                                large   _____

Lunch

Hamburger, cheese, and tomato   _____

Hot dog, beans   _____

Dinner

Fish, rice, beans, tortillas   _____

Hamburger, potatoes, squash, corn   _____

Hot dog, tomato, celery   _____

Eggs, cheese, beans, rice   _____

Dessert

Ice cream   _____

Apples and cheese   _____

Strawberries   _____

Pears   _____

Name _____

Food Origins

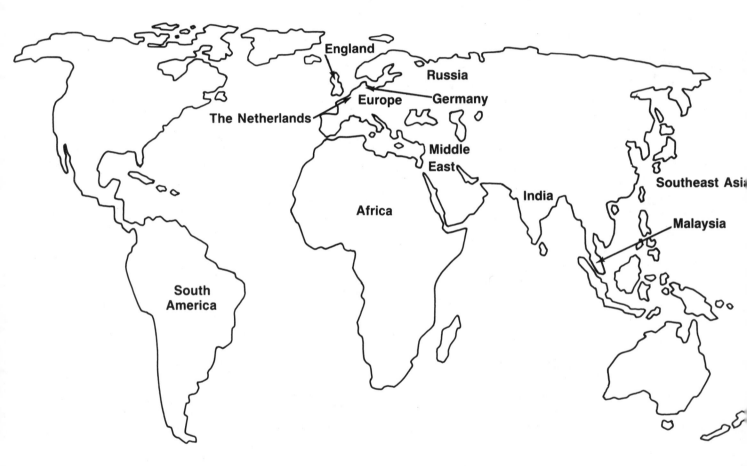

apples   Russia

bananas   Malaysia

beans   __Africa_____

carrots   _____

eggs   _____

_____   Germany

_____   Germany

milk, cheese   _____

oranges   _____

_____   _____

_____   _____

_____   _____

Unit 7: Maps

Name _____

Maps

PART 1

Left   Right

C 1st Street   B

Oak Street   Brown Street   Central Avenue   Main Street

2nd Street   A

3rd Street

4th Street

A. 1. Go 2 blocks on Main Street to 2nd Street.

2. Turn left.

3. Go 1 block to Central Avenue.

B. 1. Go 1 block on Main Street to 3rd Street.

2. Turn left.

3. Go 1 block to Central Avenue.

4. Turn right.

5. Go 2 blocks to 1st Street.

C. 1. Go 3 blocks on Main Street to 1st Street.

2. Turn left.

3. Go 3 blocks to Oak Street.

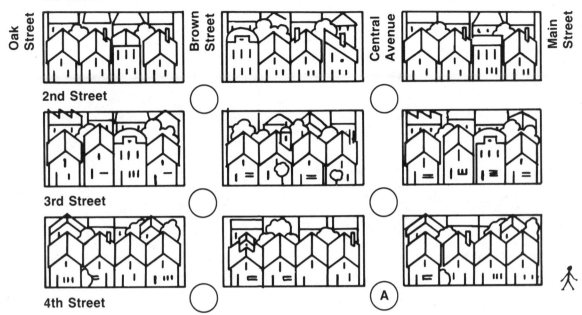

A. Go on 4th Street to Central Avenue.

B. Go on 4th Street to Brown Street.

C. 1. Go on Main Street to 3rd Street.

2. Turn left.

3. Go 2 blocks to Brown Street.

D. 1. Go on Main Street to 3rd Street.

2. Turn left.

3. Go 1 block to Central Avenue.

E. 1. Go 2 blocks on Main Street to 2nd Street.

2. Turn left.

3. Go 2 blocks to Brown Street.

F. 1. Go 2 blocks on Main Street to 2nd Street.

2. Turn left.

3. Go 1 block to Central Avenue.

PART 3

Name _____

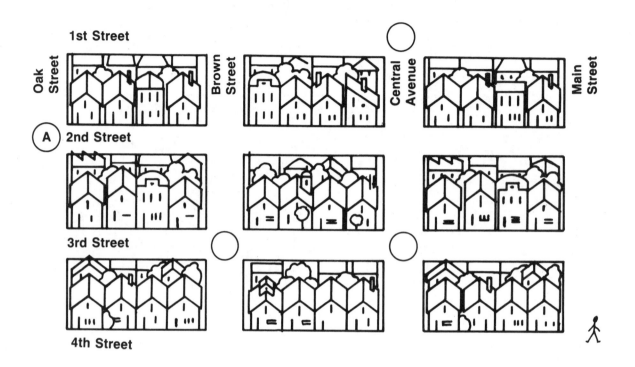

A. 1. Go on Main Street to 2nd Street.

2. Turn _____left_____.

3. Go __3__ blocks to _____Oak Street_____.

B. 1. Go on Main Street to 3rd Street.

2. Turn _____.

3. Go _____ _____ to Brown Street.

C. 1. Go on Main Street to _____ Street.

2. Turn _____.

3. Go _____ block to _____ Avenue.

D. 1. Go _____ block on _____ Street.

2. Turn _____.

3. Go _____ block to _____ Avenue.

Name _____

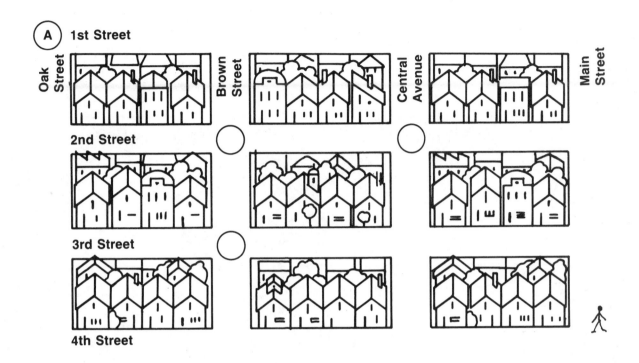

A. 1. __Go 3 blocks on Main Street to 1st Street._____

 2. _____

 3. _____

B. 1. _____

 2. _____

 3. _____

C. 1. _____

 2. _____

 3. _____

D. 1. _____

 2. _____

 3. _____

Supermarket Guide

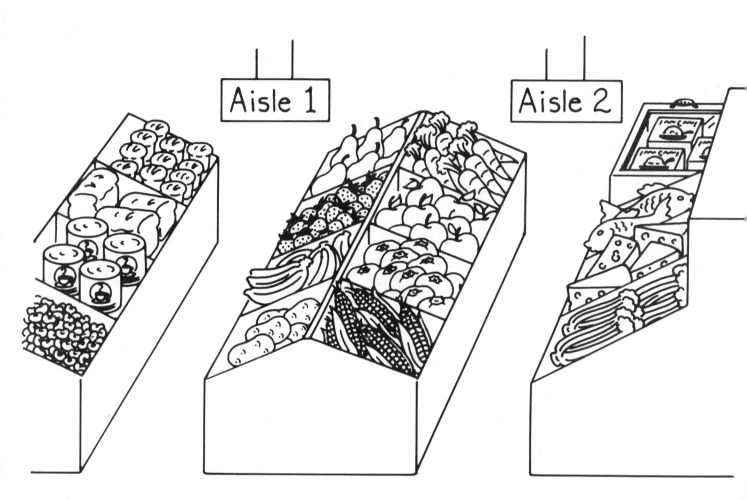

1. Where is the ice cream?

   Aisle 2, on the right.

2. Where are the muffins?

   Aisle 1, on the left.

3. Where is the bread?

   Aisle 1, on the left.

4. Where is the _____ coffee _____?

    Aisle __1__, on the ____ left ____.

5. Where is the _____?

    Aisle _____, on the _____.

6. Where is the _____?

    Aisle _____, on the _____.

7. Where are the _____?

    Aisle _____, on the _____.

8. __Where are the strawberries?_____

    Aisle _____, on the _____.

9. _____

    Aisle _____, on the _____.

10. _____

    _____

11. _____

    _____

12. _____

    _____

13. _____

    _____

14. _____

    _____

15. _____

    _____

16. _____

    _____

Unit 8: Zoo Animals

Name _____

Zoo Animals

PART 1

rhinoceros

hippopotamus

kangaroo

orangutan

flamingo

duck

zebra

turtle

goat

panda

moose

oryx

lion

seal

giraffe

rhinoceros _____   _____   _____   _____

_____   _____   _____   _____

_____   _____   _____   _____

_____   _____   _____

Name _____

Zoo Map

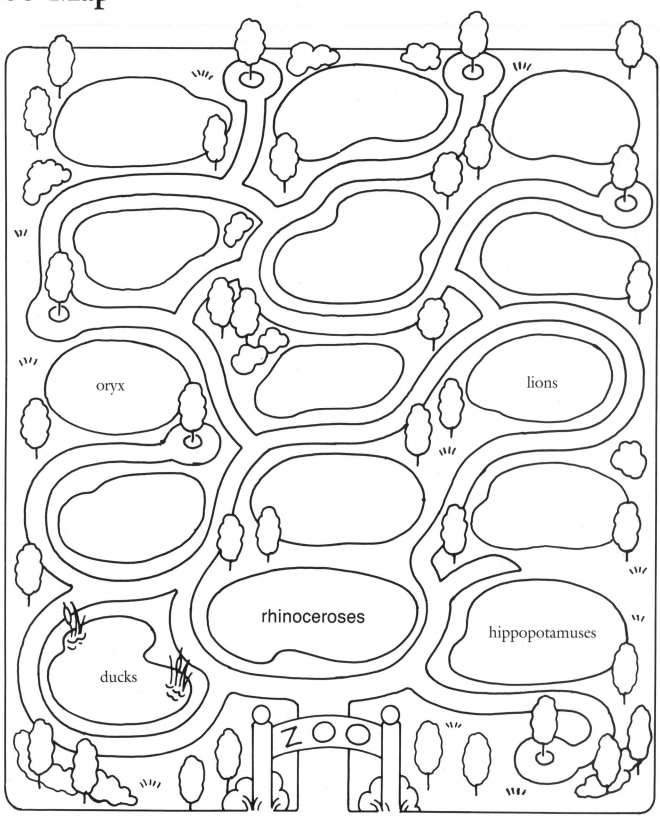

oryx

lions

rhinoceroses

hippopotamuses

ducks

ZOO

Map Directions

PART 1

1. north
2. northeast
3. east
4. southeast
5. south
6. southwest
7. west
8. northwest

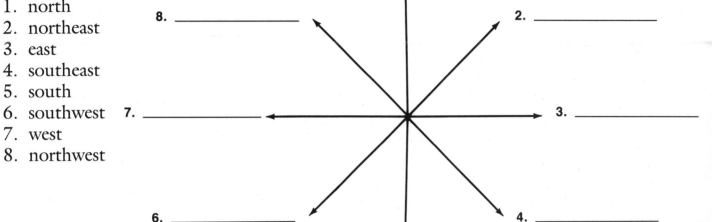

1. north

PART 2

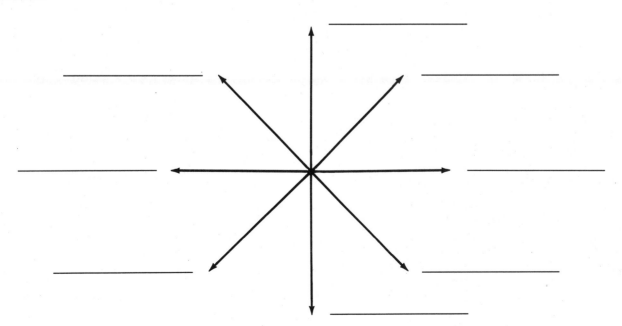

Name _____

Another Zoo Map

northwest

northeast

rhinoceroses

southwest

southeast

kangaroos

1. Where are the rhinoceroses?

   In the northeast section.

2. Where are the kangaroos?

   In the southeast section.

3. Where are the ducks?

   In the northwest section.

4. Where are the giraffes?

   In the southwest section.

5. Where are the hippopotamuses?

   In the southwest section. _____

6. Where are the orangutans?

_____

7. Where are the flamingos?

_____

8. Where are the zebras?

_____

9. Where are the turtles?

_____

10. Where are the goats?

_____

11. Where are the pandas?

_____

12. Where are the oryx?

_____

13. Where are the moose?

_____

14. Where are the lions?

_____

15. Where are the seals?

_____

Name _____

Bigger and Smaller

1. Which is bigger, a rhinoceros or a duck?

    A rhinoceros is bigger.

2. Which is smaller, a rhinoceros or a duck?

    A duck is smaller.

3. Which is bigger, a giraffe or a flamingo?

    A giraffe.

4. Which is smaller?

    A flamingo.

5. Which is bigger, a hippopotamus or a kangaroo?

    A hippopotamus is bigger.

6. Which is smaller?

    _____

7. Which is bigger, a zebra or a turtle?

    _____

8. Which is smaller?

    _____

Name _____

Zoo Animals and Their Origins

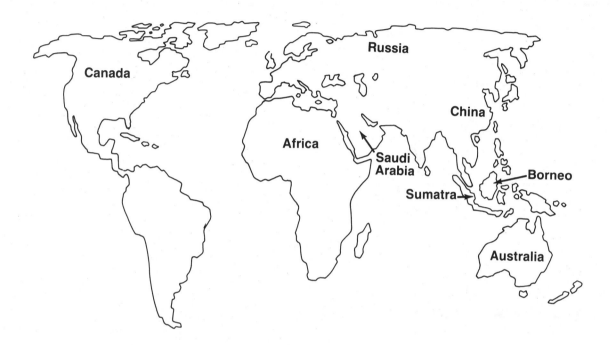

1. Where do hippopotamuses live?   <u>In Africa.</u>

2. Where do kangaroos live?   _____

3. Where do pandas live?   _____

4. Where do moose live?   _____

5. Where do lions live?   _____

6. Where do seals live?   _____

7. Where do orangutans live?   _____

8. Where do zebras live?   _____

9. Where do oryx live?   _____

Unit 9: Names, Addresses, and Phone Numbers

Name _____

Names

1. What is your name?   Diana Phomin.   Spell it, please.

   D-I-A-N-A   P-H-O-M-I-N.

2. What is your name?   Edith Wernick.   How do you spell it?

   _E_ _D_ _I_ _T_ _H_   _W_ _E_ _R_ _N_ _I_ _C_ _K_.

3. First name?   Frances, F-R-A-N-C-E-S.

   Last name?   Berger, B-E-R-G-E-R.

   Middle initial?   L.

4. What is your name?   Wendy Steiner.   Spell it.

   ____-____-____-____-____   ____-____-____-____-____-____-____.

5. What is your name?   Joe Brown.   Spell it.

   ____-____-____   ____-____-____-____-____.

6. First name?   Joe, J-O-E.   Last name?

   _____, ____-____-____-____-____.

   Middle initial?

   ____

Name _____

Phone Numbers

1. What is your phone number?   555–2066.

2. What is your phone number?   Area code (602) 555–2066.

3. What is your phone number?   555–0911.

4. And the area code?   305.

5. What is your phone number?   _____ (201) 555–2565 _____ .

6. What is your phone number?   _____ .

7. What is your phone number?   _____ .

8. What is your phone number?   _____ .

9. What is your phone number?   _____ .

10. What is your phone number?   _____ .

Area Codes

1. The area code for Montana is ___406___ .

2. The area code for South Carolina is _____ .

3. The area code for Arkansas is _____ .

4. In Nevada, the area code is _____ .

5. In Maine, the area code is _____ .

6. The area codes for Massachusetts are ___413___ and ___617___ .

7. The area codes for Florida are _____ , _____ , and _____ .

8. The area codes for Virginia are _____ and _____ .

9. In New Jersey, the area codes are _____ and _____ .

10. In California, the area codes are _____ , _____ , _____ , _____ ,

_____ , _____ , _____ , _____ , and _____ .

Name _____

Addresses

1. What is your address?

   1588 Main Street.

2. What is your address?

   1600 Main Street, Apartment 105.

3. What is your address?

   1600 Main Street, Apartment __210__.

4. What is your address?

   1600 Main Street, Apartment _____.

5. What is your address?

   _____ Main Street, Apartment _____.

6. What is your address?

   _____ Main Street.

7. What is your address? _____ Main Street.

   What number?   1632.

8. What is your address?

   _____ Main Street.

9. What is your address?

   _____ Main Street.

Name _____

Names, Addresses, and Phone Numbers

PART 1

1. Mary Bruder, M-A-R-Y B-R-U-D-E-R
   1204 Main Street
   (304) 555–8945

2. Margaret Dwyer, M-A-R-G-A-R-E-T D-W-Y-E-R
   300 Main Street
   (900) 555–7655

3. Marie Myer, M - A - R - I - E   M - Y - E - R
   2507 Central Avenue
   (301) 555–9681

4. Richard Feldman, ____ - ____ - ____ - ____ - ____ - ____ - ____

   ____ - ____ - ____ - ____ - ____ - ____ - ____

   2700 Central Avenue

   (_____) _____ - _____

5. _____ _____, ___ - ___ - ___ - ___ - ___ ___ - ___ - ___ - ___

   _____ Main Street

   (_____) _____ - _____

6. _____ _____, ___ - ___ - ___

   ___ - ___ - ___ - ___ - ___ - ___ - ___

   _____ Central Avenue

   (_____) _____ - _____

7. _____ _____, ___ - ___ - ___ - ___ - ___

   ___ - ___ - ___ - ___ - ___ - ___

   37201 Main Street

   (_____) _____ - _____

8. _____ _____, ___ - ___ - ___ - ___ - ___ - ___

   ___ - ___ - ___ - ___ - ___ - ___

   200 E. Main Street

   (_____) _____ - _____

	Name	Address	Phone Number
1.	yes	no	yes
2.			
3.			
4.			
5.			
6.			
7.			
8.			

Name _____

The Phone Book

Brown Linn 116 Central Ave 555–3409
Brown Lorie 243 Brown Rd 555–9672
Brown Louis F 6711 E. Central Ave 555–9034
Brown M 1103 Main St 555–9700
Brown M K 306 1st St 555–4500
Brown Matt and Ann 674 Main St 555–0066
Brown Norman and Adrienne 600A Oak 555–1156
Brown Pauline E 313 University 555–1154

Jones Tracy R 215 Main St. 555–3004
Jones Trudy 3119 Central Ave 555–1928
Jones Virginia C 310 Oak St 555–8884
Jones W W 3016 Central Ave 555–8923
Jones Walter 2151 Main St 555–5774
Jones William D 200 E. Main St 555–0905
Jones William F 1672 W. Main St 555–5612
Jones Willie V 5001 Central Ave 555–6688

Smith Joan 211 Central Ave 555–5081
Smith John B 23 Main St 555–2284
Smith John F 247 Central Ave 555–1006
Smith John J 964 2nd St 555–3386
Smith John L 3402 3rd St 555–7774
Smith John Lee 2206 1st St 555–7676
Smith John T 230 E. Central Ave 555–9265
Smith Johnnie 1004 Main St 555–5535

Name	Address	Phone Number
1. Linn Brown	116 Central Avenue	555–3409
2. Johnnie Smith		
3. W. W. Jones		
4. John F. Smith		
5. M. K. Brown		
6.		
7.		
8.		
9.		
10.		

Unit 10: Shapes

Name _____

Shapes

PART 1

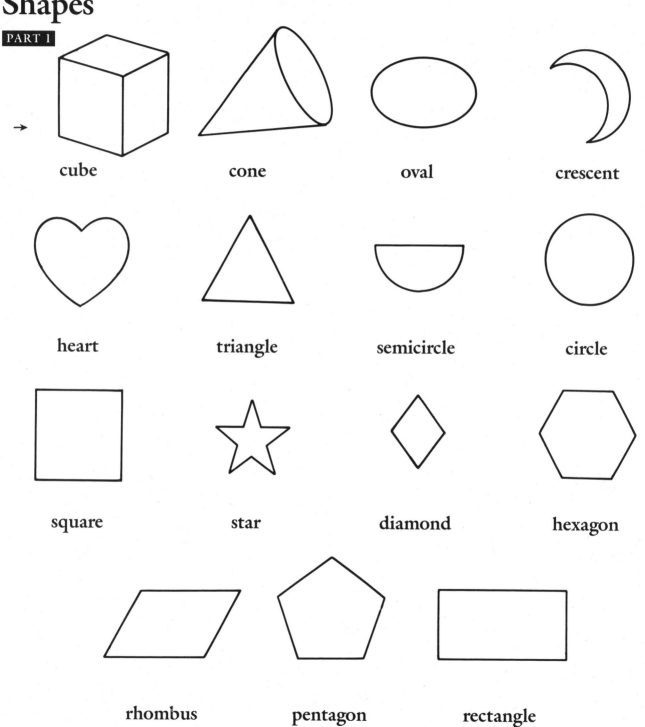

→ cube

cone

oval

crescent

heart

triangle

semicircle

circle

square

star

diamond

hexagon

rhombus

pentagon

rectangle

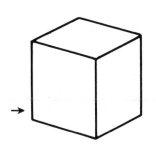 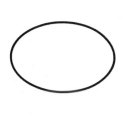 

cube _____   _____   _____   _____

  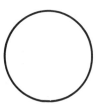

_____   _____   _____   _____

  (hexagon)

_____   _____   _____   _____

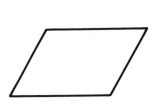 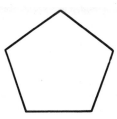 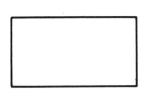

_____   _____   _____

Sides

PART 1

1. How many sides does a cube have?

    ____6____.

2. What about a triangle?

    _____.

3. A square?

    _____.

4. How about a star?

    _____.

5. A diamond?

    _____.

6. And a hexagon?

    _____.

7. What about a rhombus?

    _____.

8. And a pentagon?

    _____.

9. And a rectangle; how many sides does a rectangle have?

    _____.

Name _____

	3	4	5	6	7	8	9	10
1. __cube__				✔				
2. _____								
3. _____								
4. _____								
5. _____								
6. _____								
7. _____								
8. _____								
9. _____								

Name _____

Upper and Lower

upper left	upper right
lower left	lower right

1. Draw a cube in the upper left.

2. Draw a cone in the upper right.

3. Draw a crescent in the lower left.

4. Draw a heart in the lower right.

5. Draw a triangle in the upper right.

6. Draw a semicircle in the upper left.

7. Draw a circle in the lower right.

8. Draw a _____square_____ in the lower right.

9. Draw a _____ in the lower left.

10. Draw a _____ in the lower left.

11. Draw a _____ in the upper right.

12. Draw a _____ in the upper left.

13. Draw a _____ in the lower left.

14. Draw a _____ in the lower right.

15. Draw an _____ in the upper right.

Name _____

Top, Bottom, Right, Left, and Between

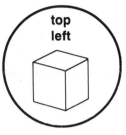
top left

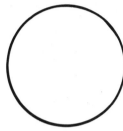

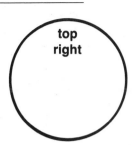
top right

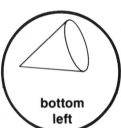

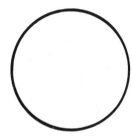

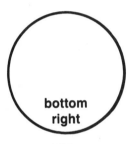

bottom left

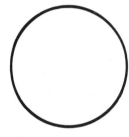
bottom right

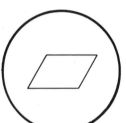

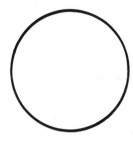

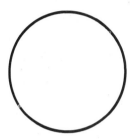

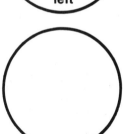

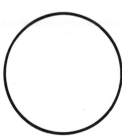

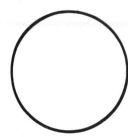

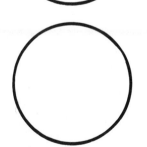

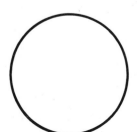

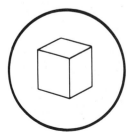

Unit 11: Linear Measurement

Name _____

Centimeters

PART 1

2 centimeters

|ıılıılıılıılı|
 1   2

___6___ centimeters

|ıılıılıılıılıılıılıılıılı|
 1   2   3   4   5   6

_____ centimeters

|ıılıılıılıılıılıılıılıılıılı|
 1   2   3   4   5   6   7

_____ centimeters

|ıılıılıılıılı|
 1   2   3

_____ centimeters

|ıılıılıılıılıılıılı|
 1   2   3   4   5

4 centimeters

|ıılıılıılıılıılıılıılı|
 1   2   3   4

_____ centimeters

|ıılıılıılı|
 1   2

_____ centimeters

|ıılıılıılıılıılıılıılıılı|
 1   2   3   4   5   6

_____ centimeters

|ıılıılıılıılıılıılı|
 1   2   3   4

_____ centimeters

|ıılıılıılıılı|
 1   2   3

1. The line is _____5_____ centimeters long.

    1   2   3   4   5

2. The pencil is _____ centimeters long.

3. The paper clip is _____ centimeters long.

4. The _____ is _____ _____ long.

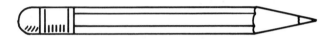

5. The _____ is _____ _____ long.

6. The _____ is _____ _____ long.

7. The _____ is _____ _____ long.

PART 3

Name _____

1. How long is the line?

   It is ___5___ centimeters long.

2. How long is the pencil?

   It is _____ centimeters long.

3. How long is the paper clip?

   _____ centimeters long.

4. How long is the _____?

   _____ centimeters.

5. How long is the _____?

   _____ centimeters.

6. How long is the _____?

   _____ _____.

7. How long is the _____?

   _____ _____.

Inches

PART 1

1. The key is ___2___ inches long.

2. The knife is _____ inches long.

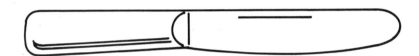

3. The brush is _____ inches long.

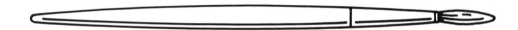

4. The _____ is _____ inches long.

_____

5. The _____ is _____ _____ long.

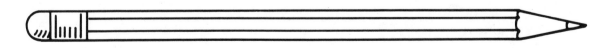

6. The _____ is _____ _____ long.

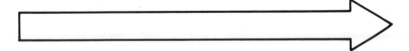

7. The _____ is _____ _____ long.

Name _____

1. How long is the key?

   It is ____2____ inches long.

2. What about the brush? How long is it?

   _____ inches long.

3. How many inches long is the _____?

   _____.

4. How long is the _____?

   _____ inches.

5. How many inches long is the _____?

   _____.

6. How long is the _____?

   _____ _____.

7. How many inches long is the _____?

   _____.

Name _____

Greater than, Less than, and Equal to

1. A 4-centimeter line is longer than a 2-centimeter line.

    ____4 cm.____   __>__   ____2 cm.____

2. A 3-centimeter line is shorter than a 6-centimeter line.

    ____3 cm.____   __<__   ____6 cm.____

3. A 5-centimeter line is equal to a 5-centimeter line.

    ____5 cm.____   __=__   ____5 cm.____

4. An 8-centimeter pencil is longer than a 5-centimeter pencil.

    _____   ____   _____

5. A 3-centimeter arrow is shorter than a 7-centimeter arrow.

    _____   ____   _____

6. A 10-centimeter line is equal to a 10-centimeter line.

    _____   ____   _____

7. A 7-centimeter line is equal to a 7-centimeter line.

    _____   ____   _____

8. A 12-centimeter pen is shorter than an 18-centimeter pen.

    _____   ____   _____

1. A 3-inch line is longer than a 2-inch line.

      __3 in.__   __>__   __2 in.__

2. A 1-inch line is shorter than a 5-inch line.

      __1 in.__   __<__   __5 in.__

3. A 3-inch line is the same length as a 3-inch line.

      __3 in.__   __=__   __3 in.__

4. A 5-inch knife is longer than a 4-inch knife.

      _____   ___   _____

5. A 7-inch brush is shorter than a 9-inch brush.

      _____   ___   _____

6. A 10-inch pencil is the same length as a 10-inch pencil.

      _____   ___   _____

7. A 3-inch key is shorter than a 4-inch key.

      _____   ___   _____

8. An 8-inch line is the same length as an 8-inch arrow.

      _____   ___   _____

Unit 12: Liquid Measurement

Name _____

Cups, Pints, Quarts, Gallons

PART 1

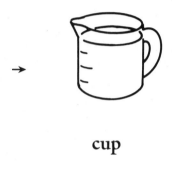

cup

pint

quart

gallon

Name _____

→

_____ cup _____

_____

_____

_____

a cup of coffee
1 cup

a bottle of milk
1 gallon

a mug of coffee
1 pint

a cup of soup
1 cup

a carton of milk
1 quart

a can of soup
1 pint

How Many?

1. How many cups in a pint?

    There are 2 cups in a pint.

2. How many cups in a quart?

    4 cups.

3. How many cups in a gallon?

    32.

4. How many pints in a quart?

    2.

5. How many pints in a gallon?

    8.

6. How many quarts in a gallon?

    4.

7. How many cups in a _____ pint _____?

    ___ 2 ___.

8. How many cups in a _____?

    _____.

9. How many _____ in a _____?

    _____.

10. How many _____ in a _____?

    _____.

11. _____

    _____.

12. _____

    _____.

Name _____

Which Is More?

PART 1

1. Which is more, a gallon or a cup?

    A gallon is more.

2. Which is more, a quart or a pint?

    A quart.

3. Which is more, 2 quarts or 1 quart?

    2 quarts.

4. Which is more, 2 pints or a gallon?

    A gallon.

PART 2

1. Which is more, a gallon or a quart?

    __A gallon._____

2. Which is more, a quart or a pint?

    _____

3. Which is more, a cup or _____?

    _____

4. Which is more, 2 pints or _____?

    _____

5. Which is more, _____?

    _____

6. _____

    _____

7. _____

    _____

8. _____

    _____

9. _____

    _____

10. _____

    _____

11. _____

    _____

Name _____

Full or Empty?

full   **empty**

1. Is the pint empty or full?

   _____ It is empty. _____

2. Is the pint empty or full?

   _____ Full. _____

3. Is the glass empty or full?

   _____

4. Is the glass empty or full?

   _____

5. Is the coffee mug empty or full?

   _____

6. Is the coffee mug empty or full?

   _____

Abbreviations

1 cup	1 pint	1 quart	1 gallon
1 c.	**1 pt.**	**1 qt.**	**1 gal.**

1. _____1 c._____

2. _____

3. _____

4. _____

Unit 13: The Body

Name _____

The Body

PART 1

eyes

nose

mouth

face

shoulders

elbow

fingers

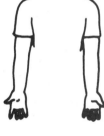
arms

legs

back

neck

ear

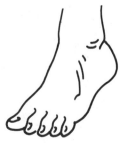
foot

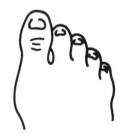
toes

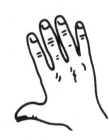
hand

knee

Name _____

_____eyes_____

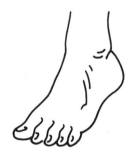   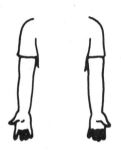

  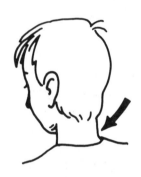 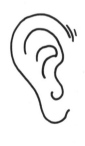

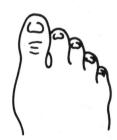 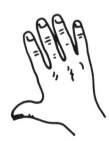  

Name _____

Limbs

  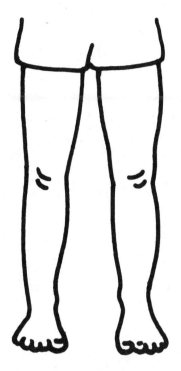

Arms   **Legs**

_____2_____ arms   _____ legs

_____ elbows   _____ knees

_____ hands   _____ feet

_____ fingers   _____ toes

Name _____

Upper or Lower?

	Upper	Lower
arms	✔	
back		
ears		
elbows		
eyes		
face		
fingers		
feet		
hands		
knees		
legs		
mouth		
neck		
nose		
shoulders		
toes		

Name _____

Parts of the Body

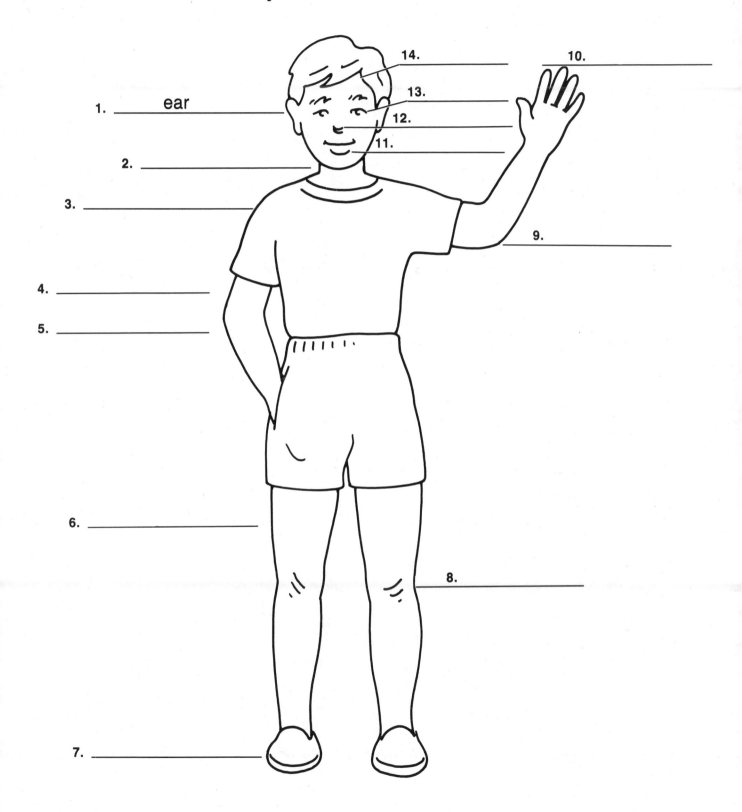

1. _____ ear _____

2. _____

3. _____

4. _____

5. _____

6. _____

7. _____

8. _____

9. _____

10. _____

11. _____

12. _____

13. _____

14. _____

Name _____

Actions

PART 1

jumping

sleeping

exercising

swimming

walking

running

reading

leaning

crawling

jumping _____   _____   _____

_____   _____   _____

_____   _____   _____

Unit 14: Clothing

Name _____

Clothing

PART 1

coat	sweater	gloves	jacket
jacket	shirt	cap	vest
scarf	sweater	blouse	pants
socks	shorts	blouse	sweater

Name _____

_____coat_____ _____ _____ _____

_____ _____ _____ _____

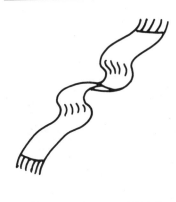 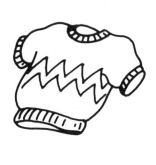  

_____ _____ _____ _____

   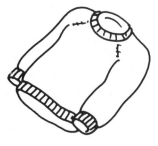

_____ _____ _____ _____

Name _____

Cold Weather or Hot Weather?

PART 1

Cold Weather

_____ coat _____

_____ jacket _____

_____

_____

_____

_____

_____

Hot Weather

_____

_____

_____

_____

Name _____

Cold Weather   Hot Weather

	Cold Weather	Hot Weather
coat	✔	
scarf		
sweater		
sweater		
gloves		
cap		
blouse		
blouse		
jacket		
socks		
shirt		
shorts		
coat		
vest		
pants		
sweater		

Name _____

Long Sleeves, Short Sleeves, or Sleeveless?

PART 1

long sleeves

short sleeves

sleeveless

Name _____

	long sleeves	short sleeves	sleeveless
coat	✔		
jacket			
jacket			
sweater			
sweater			
shirt			
shirt			
vest			
sweater			
blouse			

Name _____

Shopping for Clothes

1. blouse, short sleeves $22.99 _____

2. pants $28.00 _____

3. shirt, long sleeves _____

4. scarf _____

5. gloves _____

6. sweater, long sleeves _____

7. sweater, short sleeves _____

8. sweater, sleeveless _____

9. socks _____

10. vest _____

11. shorts _____

12. caps _____

13. jackets _____

14. coat _____

Name _____

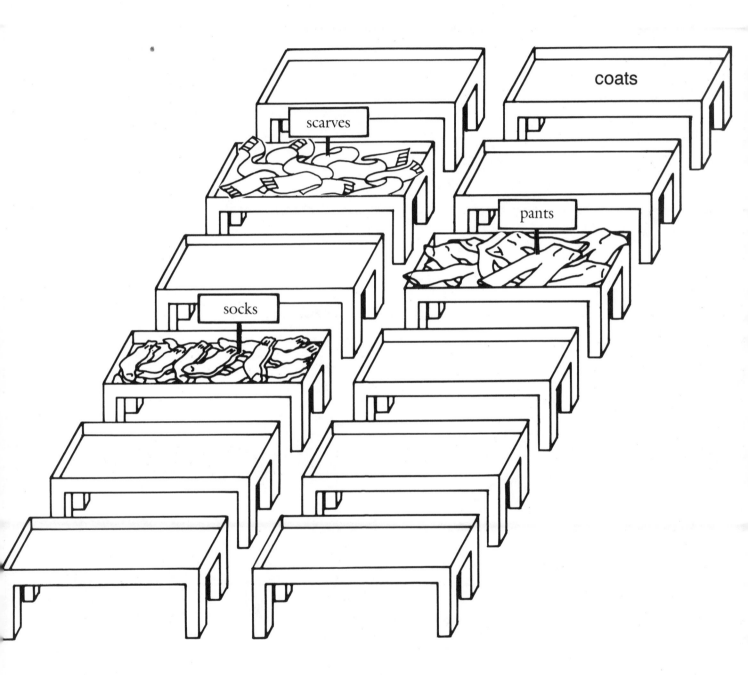

Name _____

Packing for a Trip

PART 1

Dana

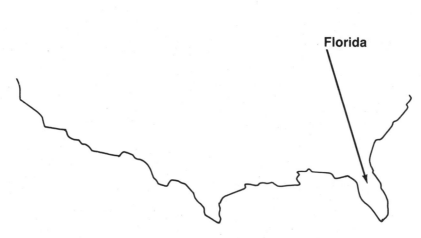

Florida

_____ sleeveless blouse _____

_____ _____ _____

Richard

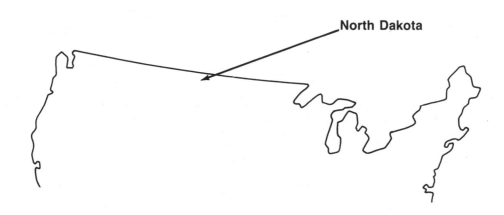

North Dakota

_____ coat _____ _____ _____

_____ _____ _____ _____

_____ _____

Dana: I'm going on a trip to Florida.

Yasuko: When are you leaving?

Dana: July 1.

Yasuko: What are you taking?

_____ sleeveless blouse _____   _____

_____   _____   _____

Richard: I'm going on a trip to North Dakota.

Steve: When are you leaving?

Richard: February 12.

Steve: What are you taking?

_____   _____   _____   _____

_____ sweaters _____   _____   _____

_____   _____

Clothing Origins

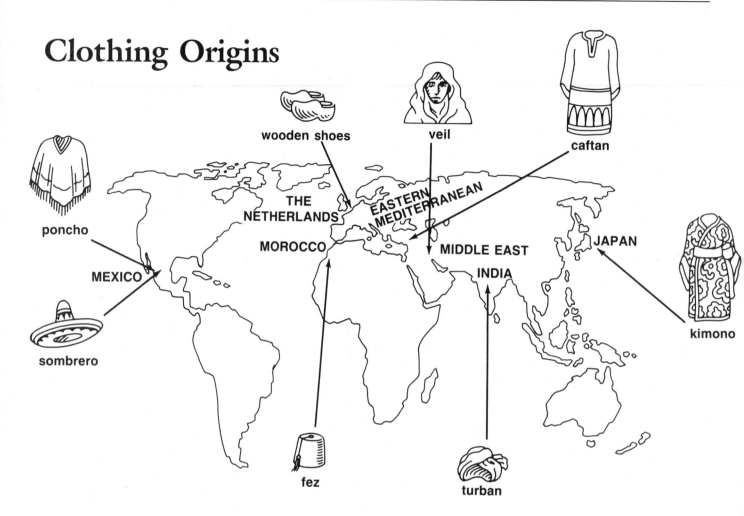

1. The _____wooden shoes_____ are from _____The Netherlands_____.

2. The _____ is from _____.

3. The _____ is from _____.

4. The _____ is from _____.

5. The _____ is from _____.

6. The _____ is from _____.

7. The _____ is from _____.

8. The _____ is from _____.

Unit 15: Musical Instruments

Name _____

Musical Instruments

PART 1

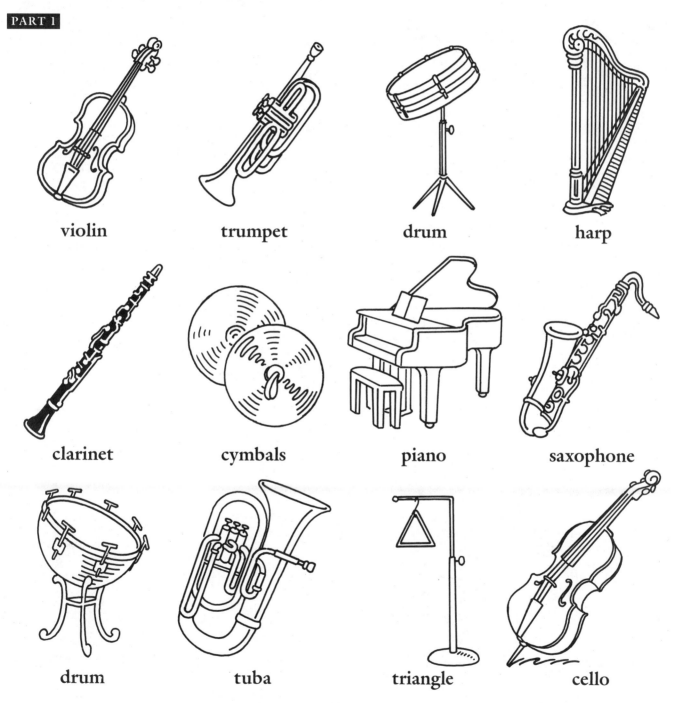

violin

trumpet

drum

harp

clarinet

cymbals

piano

saxophone

drum

tuba

triangle

cello

Name _____

→

_____violin_____ _____ _____ _____

_____ _____ _____ _____

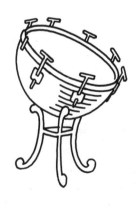  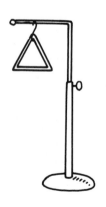 

_____ _____ _____ _____

Name _____

Instruments from Around the World

PART 1

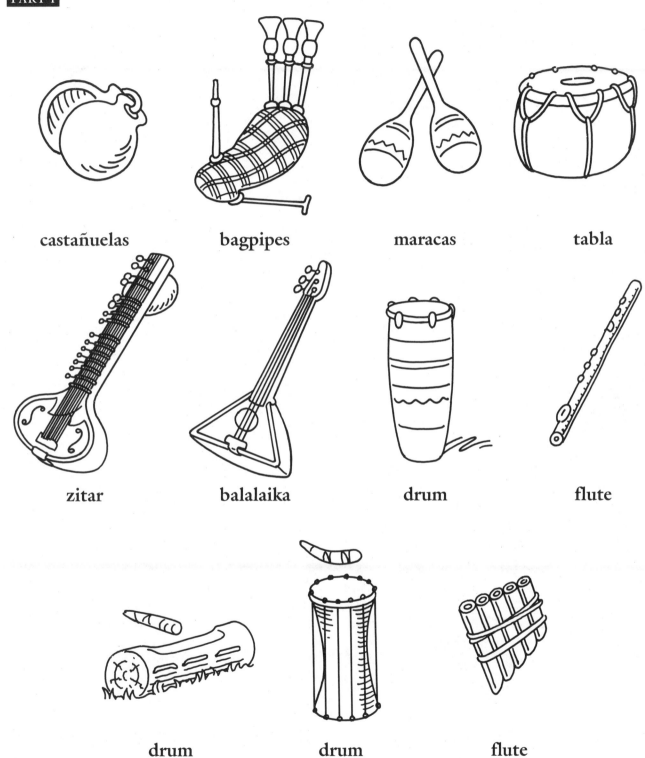

castañuelas   bagpipes   maracas   tabla

zitar   balalaika   drum   flute

drum   drum   flute

Name _____

→

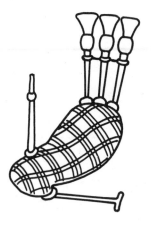

castañuelas _____ _____ _____ _____

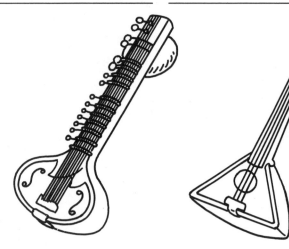

_____ _____ _____ _____

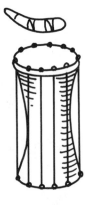

_____ _____ _____

Name _____

Sections of the Orchestra

PART 1

Wind	Percussion	Brass	String
clarinet	_____	_____	_____
_____	_____	_____	_____
	_____		
	_____		

Name _____

	Wind	Percussion	Brass	String
violin				✔
trumpet				
drums				
harp				
tuba				
saxophone				
clarinet				
cello				
cymbals				
piano				
triangle				
maracas				

Name _____

Musical Instruments and Their Origins

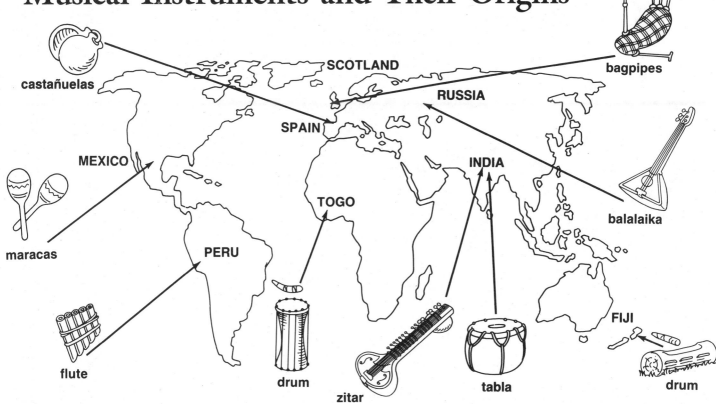

1. _____Castañuelas_____ are from _____Spain_____.

2. _____ are from _____.

3. The _____ is from _____.

4. The _____ is from _____.

5. The _____ is from _____.

6. The _____ is from _____.

7. The _____ is from _____.

8. The _____ is from _____.

9. The _____ are from _____.